Dinosaurs and Prehistoric Animals

Stegosaurus

by Helen Frost

Consulting Editor: Gail Saunders-Smith, PhD

Consultant: Jack Horner
Curator of Paleontology
Museum of the Rockies
Bozeman, Montana

Capstone
press

Mankato, Minnesota

Pebble Plus is published by Capstone Press,
151 Good Counsel Drive, P.O. Box 669, Mankato, Minnesota 56002.
www.capstonepress.com

1 2 3 4 5 6 10 09 08 07 06 05

Library of Congress Cataloging-in-Publication Data
Frost, Helen, 1949–
    Stegosaurus / by Helen Frost.
    p. cm.—(Pebble plus—dinosaurs and prehistoric animals)
    Includes bibliographical references and index.
    ISBN 0-7368-3647-0 (hardcover)
    1. Stegosaurus—Juvenile literature. I. Title. II. Series.
QE862.O65F777 2005
567.915'3—dc22   2004011092

Summary: Simple text and illustrations present stegosaurus, its body parts, and behavior.

Editorial Credits
Martha E. H. Rustad, editor; Linda Clavel, designer; Jon Hughes, illustrator; Wanda Winch, photo researcher;
    Scott Thoms, photo editor

Photo Credit
David Liebman, 20–21

The author thanks the children's library staff at the Allen County Public Library in Fort Wayne, Indiana,
for research assistance.

Note to Parents and Teachers

The Dinosaurs and Prehistoric Animals set supports national science standards related to
the evolution of life. This book describes and illustrates stegosaurus. The images support
early readers in understanding the text. The repetition of words and phrases helps early
readers learn new words. This book also introduces early readers to subject-specific
vocabulary words, which are defined in the Glossary section. Early readers may need
assistance to read some words and to use the Table of Contents, Glossary, Read More,
Internet Sites, and Index sections of the book.

Table of Contents

A Dinosaur with Plates

Stegosaurus was a dinosaur
with bony plates on its back.
The plates were shaped
like triangles.

Stegosaurus lived

in prehistoric times.

It lived about 150 million

years ago in forests

and swamps.

How Stegosaurus Looked

Stegosaurus was almost
as long as a school bus.
It was about 25 feet
(8 meters) long.

Stegosaurus had
a thick body
and a small head.

Stegosaurus had

two short front legs.

It had two long back legs.

Stegosaurus had sharp spikes on its tail. It used the spikes to protect itself.

What Stegosaurus Did

Stegosaurus walked slowly.

It drank water from streams.

Stegosaurus ate leaves
and plants. Its mouth
was shaped like a beak.

The End of Stegosaurus

Stegosaurus died out about

145 million years ago.

No one knows why

they all died. You can see

stegosaurus fossils in museums.

A Solar-Powered Dinosaur?

Glossary

beak—the hard, pointed part of an animal's mouth

dinosaur—a large reptile that lived on land in prehistoric times

forest—a large area covered with trees and plants

fossil—the remains or traces of an animal or a plant, preserved as rock

museum—a place where interesting objects of art, history, or science are shown

plate—a flat, bony growth

prehistoric—very, very old; prehistoric means belonging to a time before history was written down.

spike—a hard, pointy object; the spikes on the tail of stegosaurus were made of bone.

swamp—an area of wet, spongy ground

Read More

Cohen, Daniel. *Stegosaurus.* Discovering Dinosaurs. Mankato, Minn.: Bridgestone Books, 2001.

Dahl, Michael. *Bony Back: The Adventure of Stegosaurus.* Dinosaur World. Minneapolis: Picture Window Books, 2004.

Goecke, Michael P. *Stegosaurus.* Dinosaurs. Edina, Minn.: Abdo, 2002.

Internet Sites

FactHound offers a safe, fun way to find Internet sites related to this book. All of the sites on FactHound have been researched by our staff.

Here's how:

1. Visit *www.facthound.com*

2. Type in this special code **0736836470** for age-appropriate sites. Or enter a search word related to this book for a more general search.

3. Click on the **Fetch It** button.

FactHound will fetch the best sites for you!

Index

Word Count: 126
Grade Level: 1
Early-Intervention Level: 14

24